SCIENCE ALIVE
Living Things

Robin Kerrod

Series consultant:
Professor Eric Laithwaite

Educational consultant:
Dr Helen Rapson

Subject consultant:
Michael Boorer

Silver Burdett Press

WOODLAND PUBLIC LIBRARY

WOODLAND PUBLIC LIBRARY

D0771323

How to use this book

There are four books in the **Science Alive** series: **Moving Things, Changing Things, Living Things,** and **All Around.** They will introduce you to science in the world around you.

To find information, first look at the contents page opposite. Read the chapter list. It tells you what each page is about. You can then find the page with the information you need.

The colors on the contents page will help you to find your way through the book. Each main topic in the book is shown by a colored stripe that matches the color around the edges of the pages about that topic.

On each pair of pages inside the book, you will see this in the top right hand corner:

This shows you where to find out more about the subjects covered in those two pages. The signs tell you which of the four Science Alive books and which pages to look at.

 is the symbol for Moving Things,

 for Changing Things,

 for Living Things,

 for All Around.

You can see the symbol on the cover of each book.

For example, pages 20-21 of this book are about breathing and have these signs:

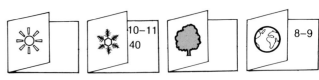

These mean: to find out more about breathing, look at pages 10–11 and 40 of Changing Things, and pages 8-9 of All Around.

On pages 37–52 of this book there are some simple activities and experiments you can try. There is a separate contents list of those on page 37, and they will help you to understand and find out more about the information in the rest of this book.

If you want to know about one particular thing, look it up in the index on page 54. For example, if you want to know about oxygen, the index tells you that there is something about it on pages 20, 21, and 53. The index also lists the pictures in the book.

When you read this book, you will find some unusual words. The first time each one is used it is written in **dark** letters. The glossary on page 53 explains what these words mean.

Note: The illustrations in this book do not show all the animals in one picture drawn to the same scale, so they do not show animals as the right size compared to each other.

CONTENTS

PLANTS AND ANIMALS

What is what?

There are millions of different things in the world around us. Some of them are alive and some are not. People, cats, flowers, and mice are alive. Rocks, water, and lumps of iron are not alive.

How can you tell a living thing from something that is not alive? One big difference is that living things can reproduce themselves. This means that they can make more of their own kind. For example, you could pick an apple from a tree, plant one of the pits, and it would grow into another apple tree. The tree is a living thing that can grow and reproduce. But you could never make a lump of iron do this.

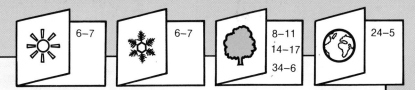
We can divide living things into two main groups — the plants and the animals. It is usually quite easy to tell whether a living thing is a plant or an animal. Most animals can move around freely, but most plants stay in the place where they grow. When you call your pet dog, it will come running to you. It is an animal. But if you called a tree in the park or garden, it would stay right where it was! It is a plant.

There is another big difference between plants and animals. Most plants can make their own food, but animals cannot. They have to eat plants or other animals.

All around us we can see living things on the land, in the water, and in the air. How many different kinds of living things can you find in the picture? Don't forget to look for little ones as well as big ones. How many are plants and how many are animals? What kinds of things can you see that are not living?

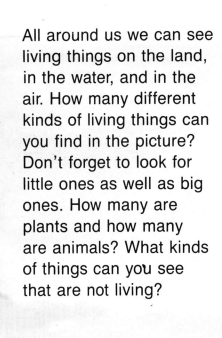

The world of plants

If you look in any garden, you will see many different plants. In summer, most of the plants have flowers, even the weeds! But in dark, damp corners you may see ferns, mosses, or toadstools. On stones or walls, you may see patches of gray, green, or yellow. These are tiny plants too, called lichens. Have you noticed that the ferns, mosses, toadstools, and lichens don't have flowers like most other plants do?

But trees can have flowers. The flowers can help to attract insects by their color and scent. The insects carry the pollen from inside one flower to the next one. In this way the insects help the plants to make seeds.

fern

mushroom, a fungus

algae

moss

These are very simple kinds of plants that do not have flowers. Fungi and molds can grow in the dark.

Inside the flowerhead the seeds are made.

The sepals protect the petals.

The petals of a flowering plant are often brightly colored to attract insects.

The stems give the plant strength.

The leaves make food for the plant.

The roots take in water for the plant. They also help keep it firmly fixed in the ground.

PARTS OF A FLOWERING PLANT

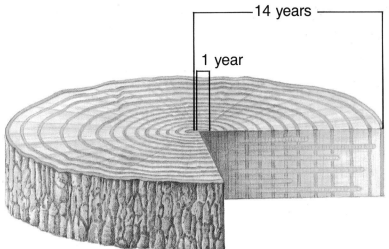

Every year in the growing season a tree grows another layer of wood around its trunk. You can see these layers as rings in the trunk.

Trees are the largest living things on Earth. This is a giant sequoia, one of the tallest kinds of tree.

Flowering plants are all made the same way. They all have roots to take in water and hold them firmly in the soil. They have stems which carry the water to the other parts. Some have branches, too. The leaves grow from the stems or the branches.

Have you also noticed that almost all the plants are green? The green coloring helps them to make food. They make food in their leaves, using the air and water around them. Green plants need to grow in the light. Without light they would turn white and no longer be able to make food. Plants like mushrooms, that have no green coloring, can't make food. Instead, they feed on the rotting leaves and wood that they grow up on. They can live in the dark.

The world of animals

What are the smallest animals you have ever seen? Perhaps they are gnats, those little black insects that wriggle over you on hot, sticky days in summer. They are so tiny you could fit quite a few on the head of a pin. What are the biggest animals you have seen? Perhaps they are giraffes or elephants. Giraffes can grow taller than a bus, and elephants can weigh more than a bus.

In between the tiny gnats and the huge elephants, there are millions of other animals of all shapes and sizes. They live different kinds of lives in different kinds of places, and eat different kinds of food.

butterfly

pigeon

bat

rabbit

rat

sea anemones

fish

spider

frog

snail

scallop

worm

turtle

There are many different kinds of animals in the world. They look different, and live differently.

lion

tiger

leopard

ocelot

wild cat

house cat

We can divide all these animals into two big groups by looking at the kind of bodies they have. If you pick up a worm, it feels soft. It has no bones in its body. A frog feels hard. It has bones, all joined to a bone in its back, that keeps its body in shape. Some animals have **backbones** like the frog, but others like the worm, don't.

There is another way to group the animals. Animals like the frog, that feel cold when you touch them, are called **cold-blooded**. Animals that feel warm, like gerbils or rabbits, are **warm-blooded**. Birds and mammals are the only animals that are warm-blooded. People are mammals, and so are cats, mice, bats, tigers, and elephants.

Some kinds of animals look alike and so we can sort them into groups. One group is the cat family.

FINDING PLANTS AND ANIMALS

Where do they live?

Do you see many sparrows where you live? You probably do, because sparrows like to live near houses and pick up the food scraps that people throw away. Do you see squirrels out in the open fields? No, squirrels like to live in trees, where they can feed on nuts and build their nests. The kind of place where animals live is called their **habitat**. The habitat of sparrows is usually the town, the habitat of squirrels is the trees.

The bodies of animals are specially made to help them live in their own habitat. Squirrels have sharp, curved claws to help them grip when they climb. They have strong back legs for jumping among the branches, and big, bushy tails to keep them steady when they jump. Moles live under the ground, and they have feet like spades for digging their tunnels. Giraffes live in dry grassland, with few plants to eat. Their long necks help them reach tree leaves.

Long-necked giraffes can eat leaves high up on trees.

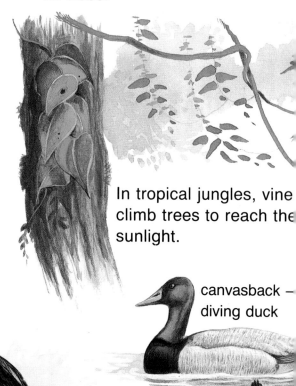

In tropical jungles, vine climb trees to reach the sunlight.

canvasback – diving duck

mallard

shoveller

dabbling ducks

Different kinds of ducks live in slightly different habitats.

red breasted merganser
sea duck — eats fish

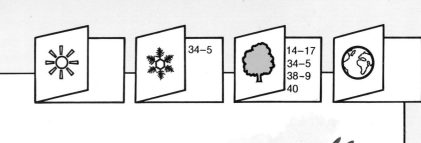

The earthworm's shape makes it easy for it to burrow through the soil.

Kestrels have very sharp eyesight that helps them see from high in the air.

Moles use their powerful legs like spades for digging.

Cacti can live in the desert because they have fleshy stems to store water.

ndarin —
rching duck

Plants like to live in certain habitats, too. Buttercups like to grow in grassy fields or on roadsides, where they can get plenty of sun. Bluebells live in the woods. They grow early in the spring, before the leaves come out on the trees and make the woods too shady. The cactus can live in the hot, dry desert because it has fleshy stems for storing any rainwater that falls.

Spotting plants

Wild plants are very interesting to study, and you can start with the wild plants we call weeds in your own garden, or a garden near you. Then you can go plant-spotting in other places. Try to visit different kinds of places, like patches of waste ground, fields, woods, ponds, thickets, or near the sea. But remember: never go on your own. Always go with a grown-up you know, and never pick any of the wild plants that you see, they might be rare or poisonous.

Take a pad and pencil with you so that you draw and write things down. When you find a new plant, write down the color of the flowers and how many petals they have. Draw the shape of the plant, the flowers and the leaves. Write down the kind of place where you found the plant.

NEVER EAT ANY PART OF A PLANT WITHOUT CHECKING IT WITH A GROWN-UP FIRST. MANY PLANTS ARE POISONOUS.

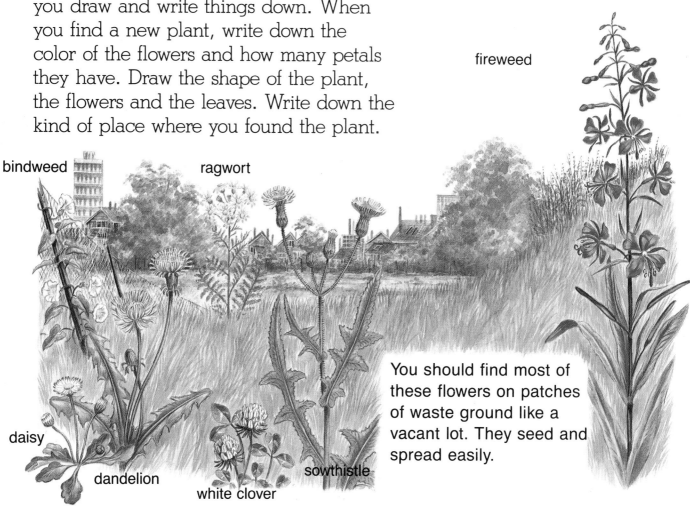

fireweed

bindweed

ragwort

daisy

dandelion

white clover

sowthistle

You should find most of these flowers on patches of waste ground like a vacant lot. They seed and spread easily.

To find the names of the plants you see, you will need books called field guides — one for wild flowers, one for trees, and perhaps one for grasses. These will have pictures of the plants and tell you their names. To find a flower in the guide, look among those that grow in the same kind of place, such as "flowers of the wood." To find a tree, look at the shape of its leaves, then find the picture of them in the book.

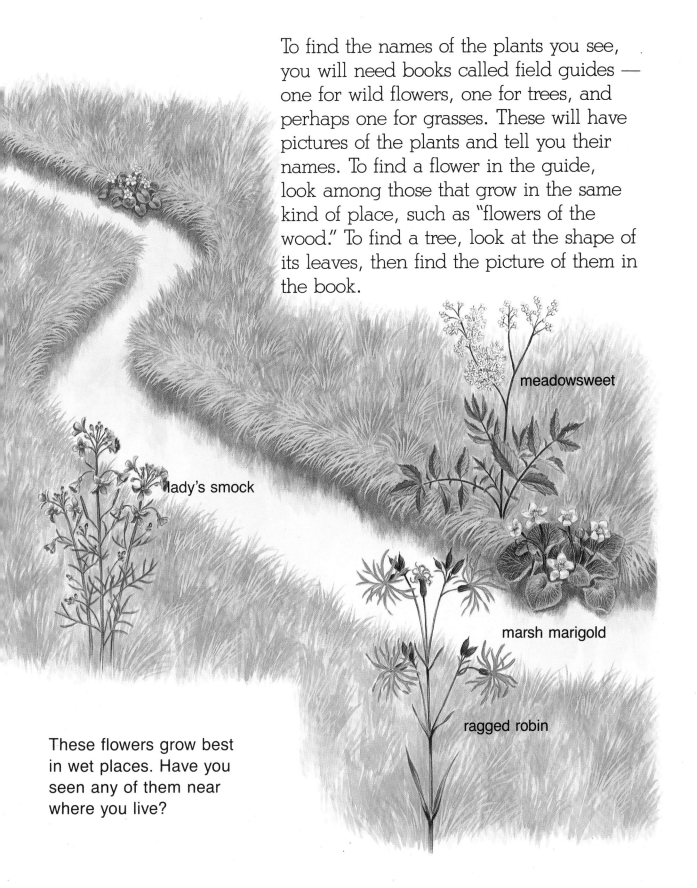

meadowsweet

lady's smock

marsh marigold

ragged robin

These flowers grow best in wet places. Have you seen any of them near where you live?

Spotting animals

You don't have to look very far to find some of the smallest animals. In the summer, flies are always buzzing around inside, and outside there are bees in the air and ladybugs, aphids, and caterpillars on the plants. Under stones, leaves, and rotting wood, there may be beetles, centipedes, woodlice, and snails. Always put back the stones, leaves, or wood after you have looked, and wash your hands, too.

Write down anything interesting you see and where you found it. Say whether it is spring, summer, autumn, or winter. Use a magnifying glass to see the animals more clearly. Can you see the feelers, or antennae, on the woodlice? How many legs does a beetle have? How many rings are there on an earthworm's body?

Look for bigger animals, too. Out in the countryside, you may see shy animals like deer. If you use binoculars, you can watch them from far away. You will need a field guide, like the ones for plants, to help you name the animals you see.

KEY

1. oak bark beetle
2. garden spider
3. crane fly
4. bumble bee
5. earwig
6. red ant
7. slug
8. snail
9. centipede
10. woodlouse

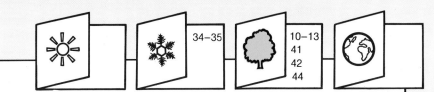

You may not always be able to see wild animals, but you might see the tracks they make. Each animal leaves a different kind of track.
Note: These animals are not all drawn to the same scale.

rabbit

hedgehog

nibbled fir cone

gray squirrel

fox

sparrow

black-headed gull

6

5

2

1

17

Feeding and growing

What are your favorite foods? Baked beans? Hamburgers? Scrambled eggs? Did you know that all these foods come from plants? Beans are part of a plant, of course. Hamburgers are made from the meat of cows, and cows feed on grass. Eggs come from chickens, and chickens feed on grain. In fact, all our food comes from plants in one way or another. Can you make a food chain for something you've eaten today, showing all the things it came from, one by one?

All plants and animals need food to grow. Plants make their own food. All they need is air, water from the soil, and light, and they can make it with the green coloring in their leaves. Without plants, people and other animals would have no food, because they can't make it themselves. The food plants make is **sugar**. They use some of it to help them grow, and turn the rest into starch and other things, which they store.

When we eat plants, our bodies break down, or digest, the things in them and turn some back into sugar. The blood carries this sugar to every part of our bodies. Our bodies use the sugar to make the energy we need to move and grow. Our bodies use the other things in plants to build and mend our bones, teeth, nails, skin, hair, flesh, and organs, like the heart and lungs.

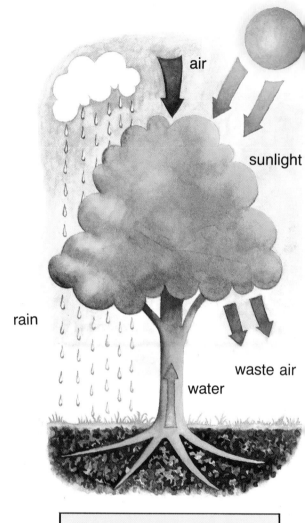

air

sunlight

rain

waste air

water

Like all green plants, a tree makes its own food. In light the leaves take in part of the air and make it join up with water to make sugar. Sugar is the tree's main food.

sheep   grass

human

Two food chains. Sheep
and rabbits feed by
eating grass and other
plants. Foxes kill rabbits
and other animals to eat.
People eat both plants
and the meat from
animals.

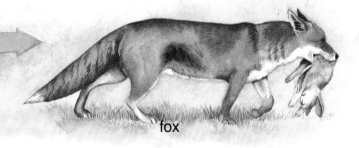

abbit

grass   fox

Some animals can eat
only one kind of food.
The cuddly-looking giant
panda eats bamboo
shoots. Only a few
pandas now remain in
the world.

Breathing

Can you think of anything you do thousands of times a day? You breathe in and out. You do this to get air into your body. There is a gas called **oxygen** in the air, and your body needs oxygen to help it work.

When you breathe in, you suck air into parts of your body called lungs. Your lungs are sort of like sponges that are full of tiny tubes of blood. The oxygen in the air goes through the tubes into your blood, and your blood carries it to all the other parts of your body. There, it joins up with the sugar in your blood, and together they make the energy you need to keep going.

When the oxygen and sugar join to make energy, they also make **carbon dioxide**. Your body does not need this, and the blood carries it back to your lungs, where it comes out as gas. Your lungs get rid of the gas when you breathe out.

hole or stoma underneath of

Plants, as well as animals, must breathe to live. They breathe through tiny holes called stomata in the underside of their leaves.

Adult insects and caterpillars breathe through tiny holes along the sides of their bodies. The holes are called spiracles.

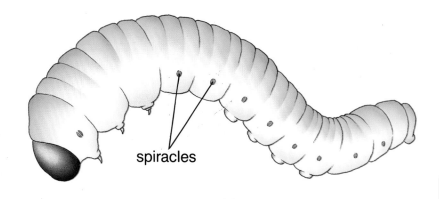

spiracles

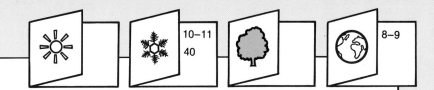
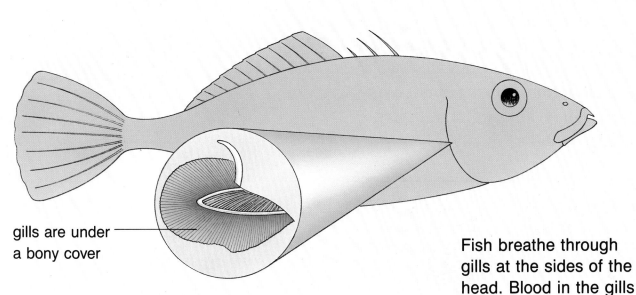

gills are under
a bony cover

All living things need oxygen to stay alive. Many animals have lungs and breathe like us, but others get their oxygen in a different way. Fish take mouthfuls of water, and the water flows through gills at the back of their heads and out through holes in their sides. As it flows through, oxygen from the water passes into the blood in the gills.

Insects take in oxygen through holes in their sides, and plants get it through holes in their leaves. Worms take in oxygen straight through their skin. But they can do this only if they are wet.

We have lungs for breathing. They have lots of blood in small tubes to collect oxygen from the air. The air travels into the lungs through the nose and mouth and windpipe.

Fish breathe through gills at the sides of the head. Blood in the gills takes in oxygen from the water passing through them.

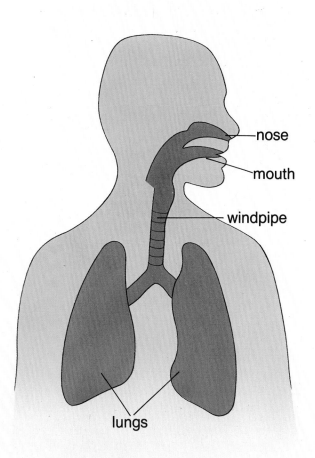

nose

mouth

windpipe

lungs

Moving

One thing almost all animals can do is move around. Like us, many animals walk on legs and feet. We have two legs. Most other big animals have four legs. Fast animals, like the cheetahs, have long legs. Slow animals, like lizards, have short legs.

Like us, birds have two legs for walking. But, instead of arms or front legs, they have wings so they can fly as well. Insects have six legs and one or two pairs of very thin wings. Spiders have eight legs, and millipedes have lots and lots. Some animals, like snakes and snails, have no legs at all. They move by wriggling their bodies against the ground.

Plants can move too, but only very slowly, when they are growing. Daisies and other flowers move their petals at night when they close them and in the morning when they open them.

Sometimes plants make very quick movements, almost like animals. When you touch the leaves of this plant they will suddenly curl up. It is known as a sensitive plant. Some plants do this to trap insects to feed on.

6–7
46
47
48

10–11

Snakes have no legs
but they can move by
pushing their bodies
against the ground.
This snake is called a
sidewinder because it
moves sideways.

Orangutans swing
through the trees on their
long, strong arms. They
use both hands and feet
for gripping the branches.

Senses

Cover up your ears, close your eyes, and hold your breath for a few seconds. Can you tell what is happening around you? Of course you can't, because you can't hear, see, or smell anything. Hearing, sight, and smell are three **senses**. They help us find out about things around us. Our other senses are touch and taste.

Most animals have senses like us. Their senses help them to find food, and warn them of danger. For most animals, sight and hearing are the two most important senses. With their eyes, they can tell where and just how far away something is. With their ears, they can tell where a sound comes from.

Hawks have very good eyesight so they can see the animal they are hunting from far away. Bats don't need good eyesight because they hunt at night.

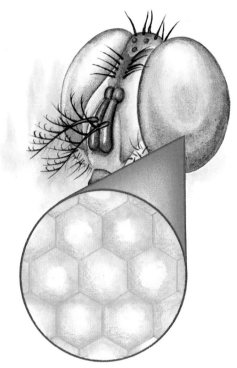

The eyes of flies are different from ours. A fly's eye is made up of many little lenses, which makes it more sensitive to movement.

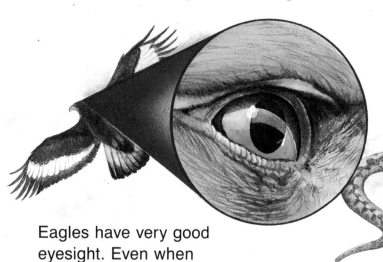

Eagles have very good eyesight. Even when they are high in the air, they can spot prey.

Snakes learn a lot with their tongues. They use them for smelling and touching.

Instead of using their eyes, bats use their ears to find the insects they want to catch. The bats make high, squeaking sounds. When the sounds hit an insect they bounce back as an echo. The bat hears the echo and can tell where the insect is.

For other animals, smell, touch, and taste are important senses. Snakes smell and touch with their tongues. That is why they flick their tongues in and out. Insects smell with their feelers, or antennae. Some insects, like flies, can even tell what something tastes like through their feet! Cats and mice can feel with their whiskers. They help the animals to find their way in the dark, when they can't see so well.

Some butterflies taste things with their feet, like many other insects. This means they can find out immediately if they like what they have landed on.

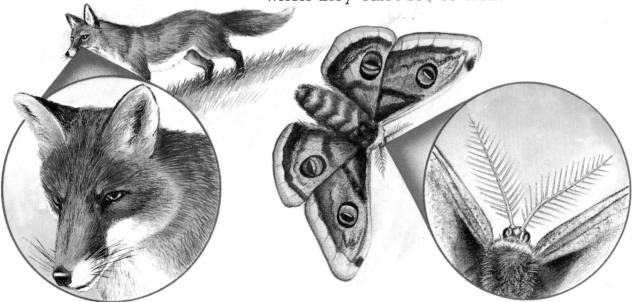

Foxes have good hearing and a good sense of smell to help them hunt.

Moths use their feathery antennae to smell things even far away.

Animal communication

Why do you think birds sing? It is not to give us pleasure but to tell other birds they are there and to warn them away. Each bird is defending its home and the area around it. We call this its **territory**.

Territory is very important to animals. In its own territory, an animal can keep any food it finds. It does not have to share with outside animals, so it has a better chance of staying alive. Animals try very hard to keep their territory. They give messages to each other by signals that other animals see or hear or smell.

In the jungle, monkeys and baboons howl, screech, and make faces at each other, as if they are going to fight. Sometimes they do fight.

People show their feelings by the expression on their faces. How do you think this football game is going?

Apes communicate with one another by making faces. This shows whether they are happy, sad, frightened, or angry. This monkey and her baby are happy.

Other animals try to look frightening in other ways. Have you ever seen what happens when two strange cats meet? They arch their backs and their hair stands up on their backs to make them look bigger. They lash their tails, show their claws, and hiss and growl. Dogs' hair stands up, too, and they growl and show their sharp teeth. But a dog wags its tail to show it is happy. Rabbits show their white tails to warn each other of danger.

Animals also use signals to attract each other when they are trying to find a mate. Have you ever seen a peacock fanning out his tail and strutting around in front of a peahen? Female moths attract mates by giving off a sort of smell that only male moths can spot.

Watch your pets, or groups of birds, and see if you can spot them giving signals to each other. If you see an ants' nest, watch how they act when one of the ants finds food such as a bread crumb.

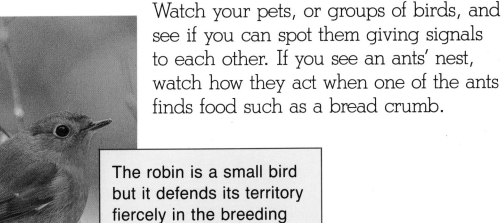

The robin is a small bird but it defends its territory fiercely in the breeding season. It puffs out its red breast and flies angrily at other birds that come near.

27

Reproduction in animals

How many animals can you think of that lay eggs? Birds do, and so do many others. This is how they have their young. It is called **reproduction**.

It takes two birds, a female and a male, to make the eggs. First, the female makes tiny eggs without a shell inside her body. The male makes something called sperm. When they mate, the male puts the sperm into the female. The sperm goes into the eggs, which then get bigger and grow shells. Then the female lays them, and sits on them to keep the eggs warm. In two or three weeks, the young birds hatch.

Frogs, fish, turtles, and insects all lay eggs. Frogs lay thousands in a kind of jelly, called frogspawn, which hatches into tadpoles. Fish can also lay thousands of eggs, but only a few of the eggs live to grow into young fish.

A green turtle lays its eggs in holes it makes in the beach. Young turtles hatch from the eggs and have to look after themselves.

A wildebeest gives birth to its baby on the African plains. The baby animal grew inside the mother's body, and will feed on milk from its mother.

Eggs are only the first stage in the life of many insects, like butterflies. Butterfly eggs hatch into caterpillars. After a time the caterpillars grow hard shells, and turn into butterflies inside them.

Mammals, such as cats, dogs, horses, and people, also make eggs and sperm, and mate. But the eggs stay inside the female's body until they have grown into baby animals. When the babies are born, the mothers make milk just to feed them. They look after their babies for quite a long time.

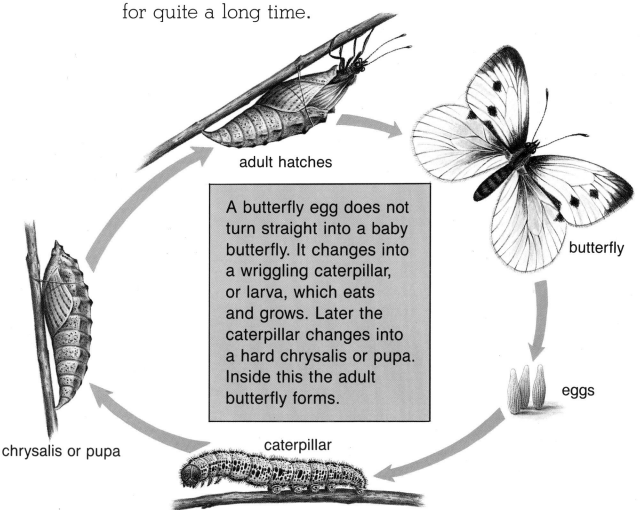

adult hatches

butterfly

A butterfly egg does not turn straight into a baby butterfly. It changes into a wriggling caterpillar, or larva, which eats and grows. Later the caterpillar changes into a hard chrysalis or pupa. Inside this the adult butterfly forms.

eggs

chrysalis or pupa

caterpillar

Reproduction in plants

Every baby has a mother and father, and most new plants also come from two parents, one female, one male. The flowers of most plants have both male and female parts. The female parts have a seed-box. The male parts, or stamens, make a sticky dust called pollen. Pollen has to fall onto the seed-box before seeds will form. This is called **pollination**. Sometimes this happens within one flower, or the wind might blow the pollen to another flower.

Some flowers attract bees and other insects with their scent and color. When the insects brush against the stamens, they get pollen on their bodies.

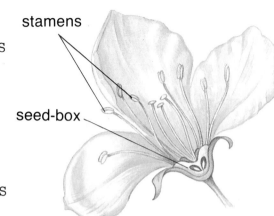

stamens

seed-box

The parts of a flower used in reproduction. The stamens make pollen, and pollen from other flowers finds its way into the seed-box where the seeds grow.

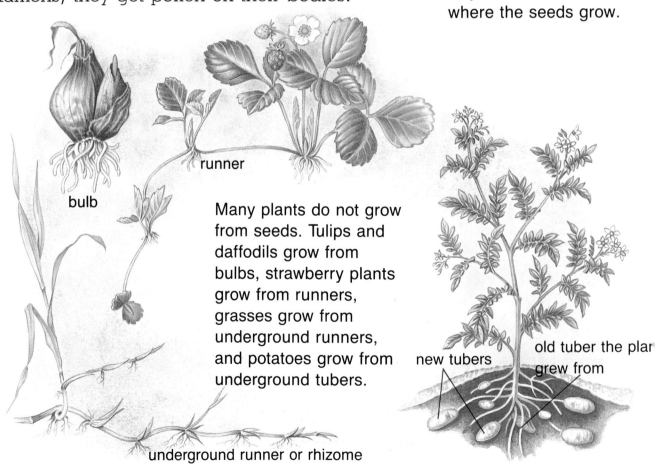

runner

bulb

Many plants do not grow from seeds. Tulips and daffodils grow from bulbs, strawberry plants grow from runners, grasses grow from underground runners, and potatoes grow from underground tubers.

new tubers

old tuber the plant grew from

underground runner or rhizome

The insects take this pollen on to the next flower. It gets into the seed-box, and the seeds begin to grow. The seed-box of the wild rose grows into a fruit we call a hip, with long, hairy seeds inside. Other plants, such as apple trees or pea plants, carry their seeds in different ways.

When birds or other animals eat fruit or berries, the seeds pass through the animals and fall to the ground to grow into new plants. The seed-boxes of other plants dry up and crack open to let the seeds out. The seeds of some trees, like the maple, have little wings on them, so they can float through the air.

Some new plants can grow in other ways. Strawberry plants grow runners with shoots on them. Where the shoots touch the ground, they grow roots and start new plants. Other plants grow from bulbs under the soil. Each year, new bulbs grow out of the first one.

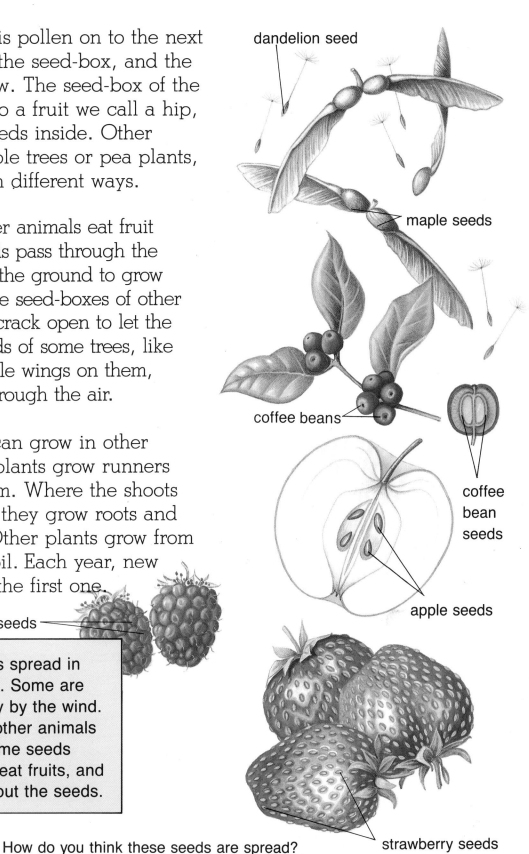

dandelion seed

maple seeds

coffee beans

coffee bean seeds

apple seeds

raspberry seeds

Plant seeds spread in many ways. Some are blown away by the wind. Birds and other animals swallow some seeds when they eat fruits, and then pass out the seeds.

How do you think these seeds are spread?

strawberry seeds

LIVING TOGETHER

Protection

Have you ever touched a nettle? If you have, you will know how much it stings. Stinging nettles are covered with fine hairs with poison in the tips. When you touch them, the poison gets into your skin. This is how nettles protect themselves from other living things that might harm them.

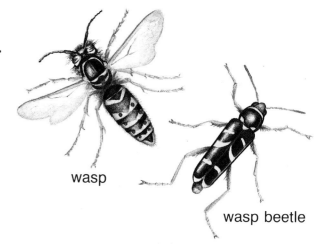

wasp

wasp beetle

Other plants have prickers or thorns to protect themselves. Blackberries have curved prickers that can tear your skin.

The harmless beetle above looks like a wasp. This helps keep its enemies away. The owl butterfly has marks on its wings which make it look like an owl and so frighten its enemies. The caterpillar's colors warn enemies that it tastes nasty.

Some animals, like porcupines, have prickers, too. These prickers are called quills. When a porcupine is frightened, it raises its quills to keep its enemies from touching it. Other animals, like turtles, have hard shells. A turtle can hide from its enemies inside its shell.

This tree trunk has a kind of lizard called a gecko on it. Can you spot the gecko? The animal is well camouflaged, and this helps protect it.

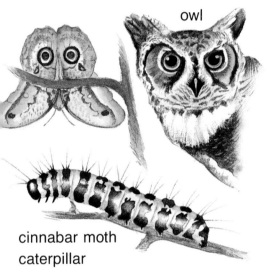

owl butterfly

owl

cinnabar moth
caterpillar

Many fish protect themselves with sharp spines. Perch have a row of spines along their backs. Porcupine fish are covered with spines and puff themselves up with water to make the spines stick out more.

Bees and wasps can sting. Ladybugs and some caterpillars are nasty to eat. All these insects have bright colors to warn other animals not to touch them. These are called **warning colors**. The hoverfly has a clever way to protect itself. It has no sting but looks like a wasp, so its enemies leave it alone. We call the hoverfly a **mimic**.

But some animals do not want to be noticed. They are the same color or pattern as the things around them so their enemies cannot easily spot them. We call this **camouflage**.

This is a kind of African antelope called an impala. It has long legs and can run very fast. It runs away when danger threatens. Its speed helps protect it.

Communities

If you watch the wildlife in a nearby woods for a long time, you will usually see the same kinds of birds and animals. They are all part of the large group, or **community**, that lies in and around the woods. The plants there are part of the community, too.

In every community, the plants and animals help one another in some way. A patch of brambles and hawthorn gives birds, like blackbirds or thrushes, a safe place to build their nests. It also gives the birds berries to eat. In turn, the birds help the plants by dropping their seeds in another place so new plants can grow. Small rodents can live in the piles of leaves that lay under brambles and hawthorn. The animals may help each other too.

The oxpecker birds eat insects that annoy the buffalo. The birds get protection from the buffalo.

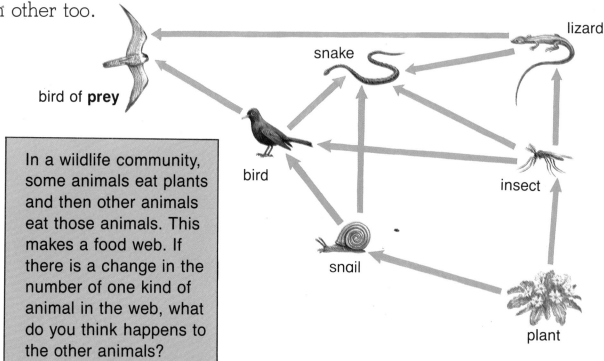

In a wildlife community, some animals eat plants and then other animals eat those animals. This makes a food web. If there is a change in the number of one kind of animal in the web, what do you think happens to the other animals?

The number of birds and animals in a community usually stays about the same. This is because there is only a certain amount of food for them all, and most have enemies that eat them. If there is plenty of food for mice one year, more of their babies will live. Then the owls that eat mice will also have more food to eat, and more babies to eat the mice. So the number of mice will fall again. In this way, the number of living things in a community is kept about the same. We call this the balance of nature.

People often change this balance. Farmers kill rabbits to stop them from eating their crops. Then there is less food for the animals that eat rabbits, so there are fewer of them, too.

This little fish is not harmed by the anemone's stinging tentacles. It protects itself from its enemies swimming inside the tentacles.

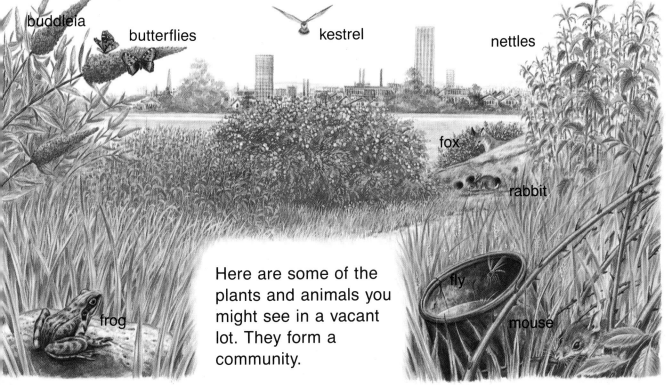

buddleia
butterflies
kestrel
nettles
fox
rabbit
fly
frog
mouse

Here are some of the plants and animals you might see in a vacant lot. They form a community.

Survival

The life of most wild animals is very hard. They have to spend a lot of time doing things just to stay alive, and to raise their young.

There are three things they must always do. First they must always be looking for food. They cannot grow food, or buy it, as we do.

Next, they must always be on the lookout for enemies that might eat them. Some animals and plants keep their enemies away with their stings, spines, or thorns. Others just run away or hide, like deer running from a lion or a turtle hiding in its shell.

Last of all, animals and plants must be able to fit in with the world around them. If the giraffe did not have a long neck, it could not reach the leaves it needs to eat.

A humming bird feeds on the sweet nectar in tropical flowers. It has a very long, thin beak that can go right into the flowers, while its wings make it hover in the air.

There is an insect in this picture but can you find it? It is a stick insect which hides from its enemies by looking like a twig.

ACTIVITY CONTENTS

Each activity has a list of things you will
need to do it, so find them and have them all
ready before you start.

Make sure you cover the table you're going to
work on with old newspaper in case of any spills.

NEVER TASTE ANYTHING you are using,
unless the book tells you to.
DON'T GO OUT ALONE TO SPOT PLANTS
AND ANIMALS IN QUIET PLACES – go with a
friend or, even better, a grown-up you know.

Many of the activities in this book are about
growing plants, and so it will take several
days, sometimes a few weeks, to get the
results. So be patient! The activities on pages
46, 47, and 48 need bean seeds that already
have a plant sprouting, so you could start off by
growing several bean seeds at once to save time.

Match the animal with its home

Animals that live in different places have different kinds of bodies. Can you match these 3 animals to the places they live in? The answers are at the bottom of this page.

A

Flat body with a hard covering. The cover has joints so the animal can bend.

B

Sleek body with paws for holding and sharp teeth for nibbling.

C

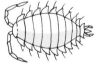

Strong legs with bristles at the edges to give a broad, paddle shape.

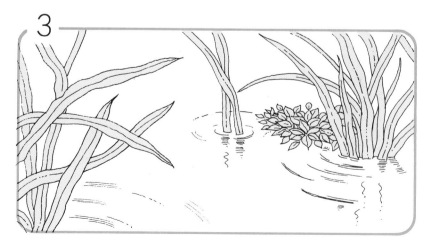

How did you decide which lives where? Did the shape of their bodies, and their legs and feet, give you a clue?

A Water boatman lives in 3
B Bank vole lives in 1
C Woodlouse lives in 2

38

Animal habitats

Every living thing likes to live in a particular kind of place, or habitat. We can try to find out which habitat some animals like best.

- A large tray or box with a well-fitting cover
- Pebbles
- Leaves
- Soil
- Some small snails

1
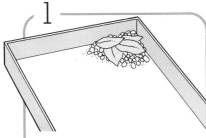
Put some dry pebbles in one corner of the tray and drop some dry leaves on top.

4
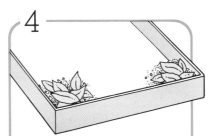
In the last corner put some wet soil with some wet leaves on top.

2
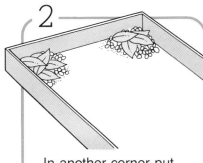
In another corner put some damp pebbles with a few wet leaves.

5
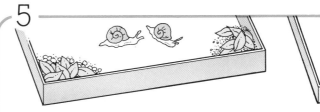
Get a few snails and put them in the middle of the tray. Put the lid on. Leave it overnight and look in the morning to see where the snails are. Did they like wet places better than dry ones? Did they like soil better than pebbles?

3
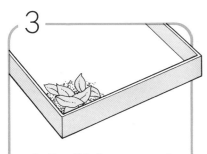
In the third corner, put some dry soil covered with dry leaves.

Try putting different things such as sand or pieces of wood in the corner, to see if there is any other habitat the snails like. Try this again with other little animals you can find in the garden, such as woodlice, beetles, and centipedes. Make sure that you always have one wet corner in your tray.

Is soil best?

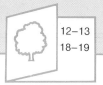

Plants will only grow well if they live in the right place. What do they need to grow in?

- Watercress seeds
- Paper towel
- Sawdust
- Sand
- Gravel
- Garden soil
- Potting soil
- Peat
- Pebbles
- Cotton
- Fallen leaves
- Empty yogurt cups with small holes in the bottom

1
Put damp paper towel to just below the top of one cup, sawdust in another, sand in another, and so on with all the things in the list above. Add some water.

2

Put a few watercress seeds into each cup.

3
Check the cups every day. Water the cups if they get dry. Write down when you plant the seeds, and when they start to sprout in each cup. Leave the seedlings in a light place and see how well each lot grows. Measure their height and see how green they look.

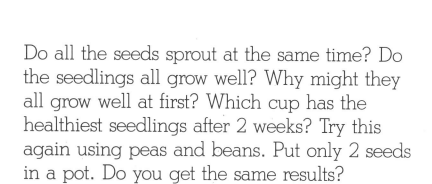

Do all the seeds sprout at the same time? Do the seedlings all grow well? Why might they all grow well at first? Which cup has the healthiest seedlings after 2 weeks? Try this again using peas and beans. Put only 2 seeds in a pot. Do you get the same results?

On the nature trail

You can learn a lot about plants and animals from books and TV programs. But nothing is quite the same as going out and watching living things in their own habitats. Don't go on your own — go with a grown-up you know.

All you really need is your senses. Use your eyes, your ears, and your nose to watch, listen, and smell. But other things can help you get even more from your outing.

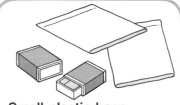

Small plastic bags and matchboxes
These are useful for carrying home leaves, grasses, eggshells, pellets, bones, and dead insects.

Notebook and pencil
These are the most important things to take, so that you can make notes and draw what you see.

Binoculars
These make far-away things seem near. With them you will be able to see small birds and other shy animals that you can't normally get close to without scaring them.

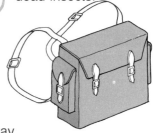

Knapsack
You will need this to carry everything. It is easier to carry a bag on your back, and it doesn't get in your way.

Magnifying glass
This is useful for looking at beetles, spiders, and other small things. You can also use it to look closely at parts of bigger animals, or at plants.

Camera
The photos you take with your camera help you remember the things you have seen and where you saw them.

If the weather is cold and wet, make sure you wear warm clothes and a raincoat and boots. If you are going to be out for a long time, you'd better take something to eat and drink as well!

Observing plants and animals

When you go plant spotting, try not to step on them, and don't pick a flower unless you can leave more than 10 around. Some wild flowers are now becoming very rare and we must leave flowers to make seeds so that new plants will grow the next year. Some states have laws to protect certain plants. So, depending on where you are it may be against the law to pick some flowers.

When you go spotting animals, you must be very quiet and patient. Then you may see some of the shy animals such as deer and kingfishers. It is a good idea to hide behind a bush so that the animals don't see you.

1

You can make yourself a "hide" from dead branches. Prop them up against one another to make a kind of bushy wigwam. Leave a hole to look through. If you are going to stay long in your hide, take a camping stool or plastic bag to sit on.

2

Make a note of anything interesting you see. Write down the date, time of day, where you see it, and what it is doing. You can use your notebook to make quick drawings of the things you see, such as the shape of a flower's leaves and petals, or an animal's track. Try to draw a plan or map showing where you see things and what is around them.

3

Field guides will help you find out what things are when you get home, or you can carry small ones with you. You will probably need several guides — on wildflowers, trees, insects, and birds.

A tree study

You can find out a lot about living things by studying a tree. Find one nearby that you can look at regularly.

- Sheets of paper
- Wax crayons
- Tape

1

Look at the leaves and see if you can find out what tree it is from a field guide. Even in the winter, when your tree might have no leaves, you can look at its shape, the kinds of buds it has on the branches, and its bark. You can often recognize a tree by its shape, its buds, and its bark.

2

To make a bark rubbing, tape a sheet of paper to the bark of the tree. Rub a crayon, on its side, against the paper. Don't press too hard. Make all the crayon strokes in the same direction. You can keep this as a record of the bark of this tree and see if you can find other trees the same.

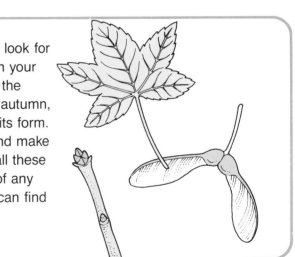

3

In the spring, look for the flowers on your tree. Then in the summer and autumn, watch the fruits form. Take notes and make drawings of all these stages, and of any animals you can find on the tree.

What kinds of birds go there and what do they do? Are there other animals in the tree? Do they find something there to eat? Look carefully into holes and cracks in the bark, look underneath the leaves and at the end of twigs. You might find that something is eating the leaves and you might see insect eggs on them, too.

Spotting animals

By trapping insects in your garden, you can find out a lot about them, where they live, and when they move about. The simplest trap to make is called a pitfall trap.

- A big yogurt cup
- A flat piece of wood
- 4 small stones

1 Dig a hole somewhere in the garden, big enough to put the cup in. Clear away the soil you dig out so the ground around looks the same as before.

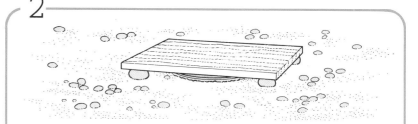

2 Fit the cup in the hole, making sure that the mouth is exactly level with the ground and that there isn't a gap around it. Put stones around the pot and rest the piece of wood on them so that there is a gap of about ¾-1 inch above the top of the cup.

Make pitfall traps in different places such as under a shrub, in a flower bed, and next to a compost heap. When you are done be sure to fill in the holes you made. (Never leave an empty hole where animals might get trapped and die.) Write down the kinds and numbers of animals you trap in each place. Are they different? Do you trap different animals at different times of day? Do you catch different ones on rainy and sunny days?

Try using an empty orange peel half instead of a pitfall trap. Put it in different places. See what you catch. Does it catch different animals from the pitfall trap?

3 Look in your trap two or three times a day. If you have caught some animals, lift out the cup. Write down the time of day and what animals you have caught, and then let them go. Put the cup back. Animals fall into the trap, but they cannot get out because the sides are too steep and slippery.

Feeding and growing

Why don't plants grow in deep caves? What is missing there that plants need?

- Watercress seeds
- Empty yogurt cups
- Potting soil
- A sheet of black paper or a piece of cardboard

1 Half-fill two cups with damp potting soil and sow a few seeds in each. Put them on a windowsill.

2 Cover one of the cups with a piece of black paper. Check the cups every day to see if they need watering.

Do the seeds sprout in both cups? Let the seedlings grow. Keep the black paper covering one cup. What happens in each cup? Do all the seedlings grow strong and healthy?

Try planting seeds again in two cups. Use damp soil in one, dry in the other. Keep them both in the light but only water the damp one. What happens this time? What do plants need to grow?

Plant movement

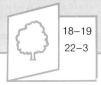
What makes a plant move, or grow, in a certain direction?

- A bean seed
- A yogurt cup
- Potting soil
- A cardboard box
- Pieces of cardboard from a cereal box
- Tape

1

Soak the bean seed in water overnight. The next day, fill the yogurt cup with damp soil and plant the bean about ½ inch below the soil's surface.

2

Keep the soil damp. Once the bean has a shoot growing up, make a maze inside the shoe box by fixing 2 pieces of cardboard inside it with tape. The cardboard should stick out just over half-way across.

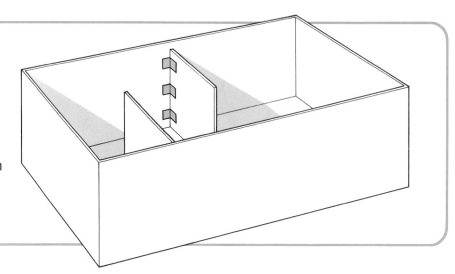

3

Cut a hole about 1 inch wide in one end of the box, and put the bean in its cup at the other end. Put the lid on the box and leave it so that sunlight shines in through the hole. What do you see happening after about a week?

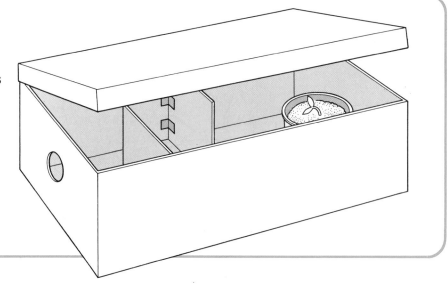

Where do roots go?

Do some parts of plants grow and move in certain directions?

- A glass or clear plastic jar with a lid
- Cotton or sawdust
- Bean seeds
- Dark paper or black plastic
- Tape

1

Fill a jar with cotton or sawdust.
Push 2 or 3 bean seeds down the sides of the jar. Water the jar to keep the cotton or sawdust moist. Fix dark paper or plastic around the jar.

2

After a few days the beans will begin to shoot. Which way do the shoots go? Are there any roots? Which way do they grow?

3

Let the roots grow to the bottom of the jar and then put on the lid and turn the jar upside down. What happens to the roots after a few days? Turn the jar the right way up again. What happens.?

Do the roots always grow the same way? What happens to the shoots?

Toward water

Plants need water to grow. Will they try to find it?

- 10 beans soaked overnight
- Sawdust or cotton
- A jar
- A large plastic box or cookie tin
- A pottery plant pot and a cork to block the hole in it

1 Plant some bean seeds in damp sawdust in a jar until they grow roots.

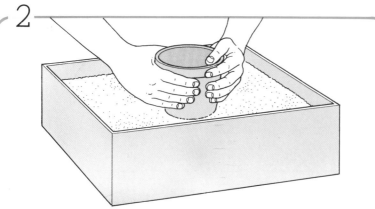

2 Fill a large cookie tin with dry sawdust. Push the cork into the hole in the bottom of a small pottery plant pot. Push the pot down into the sawdust, then fill it with water.

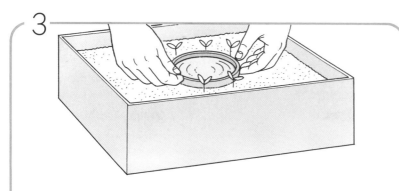

3 Plant the beans in the sawdust around the water pot.

After a few days, carefully brush away the sawdust from around the beans. What do you see? Move the beans around, and then leave them again for a few days. Do the roots change direction? Why?

Senses

We learn all about the world around us with our eyes, ears, nose, tongue, and skin. These parts of our bodies give us our senses of sight, hearing, smell, taste, and touch. How good is your sight? Can it be tricked?

1

Hold the book in front of your face at arm's length, and close your left eye. Look at the black dot with your right eye. Can you see the cross? Keep looking at the black dot and pull the book slowly toward you. What happens to the cross?

●

Did the cross disappear? It's still there, of course, but you can't see it. The reason is that the light coming to your eye from the cross has fallen on part of the inside of your eye which cannot see things. This blind spot is where the nerve goes from the eye to your brain.

2

Close your left eye. In front of you hold up a small coin in your left hand and a bigger coin in your right. Keep looking at the coins, and move the bigger coin away from you until both coins seem to be the same size. Your eye is fooling you isn't it? Open your left eye. How do the coins look now?

Looking at things with two eyes gives you a sense of distance. Your brain can work out what is smaller or larger.

Senses

3

But even two eyes can easily fool you. Hold up your hands level with your eyes and with the tips of your first fingers touching. Move your fingers toward you but look past them into the distance. What seems to be between your fingers?

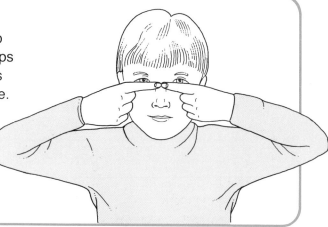

Sweet and sour

You taste with your tongue, but not every part of your tongue is sensitive to the same things.

- Sugar
- Salt
- Lemon juice
- Paper and pencil

1

Wash your hands. Dip one finger into a little sugar. Touch your finger onto the front, the back, the middle, and the sides of your tongue. Does the sugar taste sweet everywhere?

2

Do this again using some salt. Where on the tongue does the salt taste saltiest? Do the same thing with lemon juice. Where does that taste sourest?

Make a taste map of your tongue. Draw the shape of your tongue and mark in the main taste areas showing where each thing — sweet, sour, or salty — tastes strongest. Does the middle of your tongue taste anything?

Taking cuttings

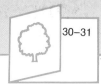

You can often grow new plants from cuttings. These are pieces cut off another plant. It is easy to take cuttings of many house plants. But take a few at the same time because some may not grow.

- A house plant
- Scissors
- Empty yogurt cups
- Potting soil

1 Cut a young shoot with four or five leaves on it, from a house plant. Make the cut just below a leaf.

2 Cut off the leaves at the bottom of the stems, and stand the cuttings in water. Leave them for 10–14 days. What happens?

3

Make a few drainage holes in the bottom of the yogurt cups with your scissors. Once the cuttings have roots, carefully plant them in damp potting soil, making sure you don't break off the roots. The cuttings should grow well. Keep the soil damp.

You can grow new spider plants from the little plants growing on the ends of long white stems. Just cut off the stem and put the small plant right into damp potting soil.

Try planting a leaf from an African violet. Put the stalk of the leaf in soil right up to the leaf blade. How many plants grow from one leaf?

Growing a tree

You can try growing your own tree from the seeds of fruit you have eaten.

- Orange, tangerine, or lemon pits
- Jar
- Small pebbles
- Potting soil
- A plastic bag
- An elastic band
- Plant pots

1

Put a layer of small pebbles in the bottom of the jar. Cover them with a layer of soil.

2

Push two or three pits just below the top of the soil and water it gently.

3

Put the jar inside the plastic bag and fasten it. Leave the jar in a warm place.

4

Once you have plants with leaves, plant them out in separate pots, and put them in the light.

Look carefully at your trees as they grow. Are all the leaves the same as the first two leaves that grow? These are called the seed leaves. Try using seeds from other trees, such as acorns or maple seeds.

GLOSSARY

A glossary is a word list. This one explains the unusual words that are used in this book.

Backbone Your body's main bone which runs down the middle of your back. It is the main support in your body, but is made of smaller bones so it will bend.

Camouflage Colors or patterns which make plants and animals fade into their background so they can't be seen by their enemies.

Carbon dioxide The gas that living things give out when they breathe.

Cold-blooded An animal whose body is at the same temperature as its surroundings.

Community The group of plants and animals that live together in one place.

Habitat The kind of place where a plant or animal likes to live.

Mammals The most advanced kind of animal. Female mammals feed their babies on their own milk.

Mimic A harmless animal which protects itself by looking like a dangerous one.

Oxygen The gas in the air which all living things must breathe to live.

Pollination This happens when the pollen from the male part of a flower goes into the female part, often in another flower.

Prey An animal which another animal hunts for food.

Reproduction The way a living thing makes more of its own kind.

Senses The way animals find out about the world around them. The main senses are sight, hearing, smell, touch, and taste.

Sugar The main food of plants, and also important for animals. They use the sugar to give them energy to grow and move.

Territory The area in which an animal lives and raises its young.

Warm-blooded Animals with blood that always stays at about the same temperature. They do not rely on the sun to warm them.

Warning color Some creatures have a vivid color that warns other animals of nasty surprises, such as that they are unpleasant to eat, or that they can sting.

INDEX

The **dark** numbers tell you where you will find a picture of the subject.